A Smart Kid's Guide to
Internet Privacy

David J. Jakubiak

PowerKiDS
press
New York

Published in 2010 by The Rosen Publishing Group, Inc.
29 East 21st Street, New York, NY 10010

First Edition

Editor: Amelie von Zumbusch
Book Design: Julio Gil
Photo Researcher: Jessica Gerweck

Photo Credits: Cover Bruce Laurance/Getty Images; p. 5 John Kelly/Getty Images; p. 6 © Rick Barrentine/Corbis; p. 9 © LWA-Dann Tardif/Corbis; p. 10 Christa Renee/Getty Images; p.13 © JLP/Jose L. Pelaez/Corbis; p. 14 MacGregor & Gordon/Getty Images; p. 17 © Tim Tadder/Corbis; p. 18 Shutterstock.com; p. 21© Hill Street Studios/Stock This Way/Corbis.

Library of Congress Cataloging-in-Publication Data

Jakubiak, David J.
  A smart kid's guide to Internet privacy / David J. Jakubiak. — 1st ed.
    p. cm. — (Kids online)
  Includes bibliographical references and index.
  ISBN 978-1-4042-8118-9 (library binding) — ISBN 978-1-4358-3356-2 (pbk.) — ISBN 978-1-4358-3357-9 (6-pack)
  1. Internet—Safety measures—Juvenile literature. 2. Internet and children—Juvenile literature. 3. Spyware (Computer software—Juvenile literature. 4. Computer crimes—Prevention—Juvenile literature. 5. Privacy, Right to—Juvenile literature. I. Title.
  HQ784.I58.J362 2010
  005.8—dc22

                              2009005369

Manufactured in the United States of America
CPSIA Compliance Information: Batch # CR110380: For Further Information Contact Rosen Publishing, New York, New York at 1-800-237-9932

Contents

Why Do We Need Privacy?

If you had a window that looked out over the whole world, would you look through it? What if using it meant that the whole world could look through back at you? The Internet is like a window to the world. It brings together people from all over. Many people online just want to learn and to have fun. However, some people use the Internet to steal from or hurt other people.

You can **protect** yourself from these people. Keep your personal **information**, such as your **screen name** and birthday, private. If untrustworthy people cannot learn anything about you, it will be harder for them to hurt you. Making sure that your information cannot be found online is called Internet privacy.

The Internet lets people around the world get in touch with you, even when you are using a computer in the privacy of your own room.

When you pick a password, try to come up with something that will be hard for others to guess. Never use your address, birthday, or phone number in your password.

Protect Yourself

Never send personal information by e-mail. Do not post it on a Web site, either. Never let anyone online know your name, age, or address. Keep the names of your school and sports teams private, too. Make sure that your screen names and **passwords** do not hold clues to your personal information, either.

Use your imagination when picking passwords. A mix of capital and lowercase letters, **symbols**, and numbers can make your password one of a kind. This mix also makes your password safe because it is hard to guess. If your password is "slam dunk," try changing it to "$1@mdUnK!" Write your passwords down and hide them somewhere away from your computer.

E-Mail Safety

Your e-mail can seem like your own private mailbox on the Internet. However, if you are not careful, anyone can read your messages. This can happen if someone finds out your password. People who know your password can even send e-mails pretending to be you!

Keeping your e-mail password to yourself is very important. Your password lets you get into your e-mail, where you can read and send messages. One way to stay safe is to change your password every few months. Every so often, **delete** all your old messages. Be sure to delete your sent e-mails, too. If someone still gets into your e-mail, tell an adult.

E-mail is a fun and easy way to keep in touch with friends and relatives in far-off places. As long as you are careful, e-mail is also generally safe.

9

Do not believe everything you read in a junk e-mail. Junk e-mails are often sent by people who are trying to mislead you or get you to buy something.

Junk Mail

Always be careful about which e-mails you open. Open e-mails only from people you know. If you get an **attachment**, ask an adult before opening it.

There are several kinds of troublesome e-mails. Spam messages are e-mails that offer you things you did not ask for and do not need. They can make your e-mail send unwanted messages to other people. Delete these messages without reading them. Phishing schemes send e-mails that use lies to trick you. They may look like e-mails from a trustworthy place, such as a bank or social networking site. However, they ask you to send personal information that can be used to steal from you.

Privacy in Postings

If you become part of online chats or have a **blog** or Web site, you will need to pay special attention to protecting your privacy. Some chat rooms and Web sites may ask for information you are not supposed to share online, such as your real name and where you go to school. A chat room may want to post your e-mail address next to every message. Sites that people pay to join may even ask you to enter your parent's credit card information. Never put this kind of information online without talking to a parent.

If a site wants you to give up your privacy, you should not use that site. Instead, ask a teacher or librarian to help you find a site that is safe and that cares about your privacy.

Blogs and chat rooms give you the chance to share your thoughts and feelings online. Make sure not to share personal information, though!

Web sites may leave cookies on school
and library computers, too. A teacher or librarian can show
you how to get rid of these cookies.

Be Aware of Spyware

When you visit certain Web sites, they leave things called cookies on your computer. Cookies help your computer remember things, such as passwords. However, cookies also let the Web sites that left them know what other Web sites you visit and what videos you watch online.

Some sites also use a tool called spyware. Spyware tracks your Internet use. Some spyware can even track the keys you type on your keyboard. Companies with spyware generally use this **data** to try to sell you things. Thieves use spyware to try to steal passwords. You can avoid spyware by not adding new applications to your computer, even if a site says they are safe.

Blocking Online Predators

Some people use the Internet to trick children. Online predators pretend to be your friend. However, they ask you to do things that are illegal. If someone you do not know tries to **contact** you on a message board, do not answer. If somebody asks you to send him or her pictures of yourself or sends you bad pictures, tell an adult. The things that online predators do are against the law, so the adult may need to call the police.

If an online predator sends you a message, it is not your fault. Do not let the predator make you feel like you are the one who is to blame. The online predator is the one who has done something wrong.

Getting a message from an online predator
can make you feel scared and alone. If you hear from a predator,
do not keep it to yourself. Tell a trusted adult.

Do not write anything about your friends online without checking with them first. Good friends protect each other's Internet privacy.

Clearing Your Name

There may be times when you discover that your personal information is listed online. The information might be there because you made a mistake and put it online. A friend may have made a bad choice and posted your e-mail address on the Web, too. Bullies also sometimes put other people's information online on purpose.

If this happens, ask for help removing the information from the Web site. Talk to an adult, such as your mother, father, or teacher. Your computer's **preferences** menu may let you clear a Web page. An adult may have to contact the site to have the information taken off. Do not be scared or **ignore** the problem, though. Act fast and fix it.

Looking Out for Your Privacy

If you are younger than 13 years old, there is a law that protects your online privacy. The Children's Online Privacy Protection Act of 1998 makes it illegal for Web sites to gather information about you, unless your parents say it is all right. The law also lets parents track what information Web sites have gathered about their kids.

This law puts your parents in charge of your online privacy. That means that when your parents check what you are up to online, they are just doing what they are supposed to do. Make your parents' job a little easier by being smart about your personal information. Internet privacy is important!

Spending time online with your mom
or dad is a good idea. It will give your parent a chance to see how
you are protecting your privacy online.

21

Safety Tips

- Have a parent help you make a list of your personal information so that you will know what to keep private.

- Find a safe spot in which to hide your passwords. Your backpack is not safe enough!

- Never click on links that offer you money or prizes.

- Set up your e-mail to receive messages only from people who are in your address book.

- **Bookmark** safe sites that do not use cookies or put spyware on your computer.

- Make a list of "Computer Dos and Don'ts" to hang near your computer.

- Use different passwords for different sites.

- Have an adult use tools on your computer to look for and get rid of any cookies you may have picked up online.

Glossary

attachment (uh-TACH-mint) An extra part of an e-mail that you must click on to open.

blog (BLOG) A Web site where people share thoughts and facts.

bookmark (BUHK-mahrk) To save the addresses of Web sites in a browser.

contact (KON-takt) To talk or meet with a person.

data (DAY-tuh) Facts.

delete (dih-LEET) To erase or get rid of totally.

ignore (ig-NOR) To pay no attention to something.

information (in-fer-MAY-shun) Knowledge or facts.

passwords (PAS-wurdz) Secret combinations of letters or numbers that let people enter something.

preferences (PREH-fernts-ez) Things people pick about a computer's setup.

protect (pruh-TEKT) To keep safe.

screen name (SKREEN NAYM) A name someone uses online.

symbols (SIM-bulz) Objects or pictures that stand for something else.

Index

Web Sites

Due to the changing nature of Internet links, PowerKids Press has developed an online list of Web sites related to the subject of this book. This site is updated regularly. Please use this link to access the list: www.powerkidslinks.com/onlin/privacy/